KEMETIC HOLISTIC LIFE COACH HAND BOOK 101 REVISED EDITION

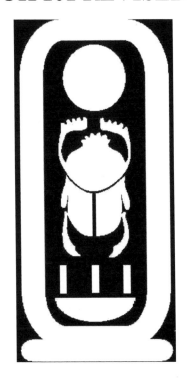

I AM BECOMING

By Faheem Judah-EL D.D.

KEMETIC SACRED LIFE ASSOCIATION

"Speak to us of Love."

And he raised his head and looked upon the people, and there fell a stillness upon them. And with a great voice he said:

"When love beckons to you follow him, though his ways are hard and steep. And when his wings enfold you yield to him, though the sword hidden among his pinions may wound you. And when he speaks to you believe in him, though his voice may shatter your dreams as the north wind lays waste the garden. For even as love crowns you so shall he crucify you. Even as he is for your growth so is he for your pruning. Even as he ascends to your height and caresses your tenderest branches that quiver in the sun, so shall he descend to your roots and shake them in their clinging to the earth. Like sheaves of corn he gathers you unto himself.

He threshes you to make you naked.

He sifts you to free you from your husks.

He grinds you to whiteness.

He kneads you until you are pliant;

And then he assigns you to his sacred fire, that you may become sacred bread for God's sacred feast. All these things shall love do unto you that you may know the secrets of your heart and in that knowledge become a fragment of Life's heart. But if in your fear you would seek only love's peace and love's pleasure, then it is better for you that you cover your nakedness and pass out of love's threshing-floor, into the seasonless world where you shall laugh, but not all of your laughter, and weep, but not all of your tears.

Love gives naught but itself and takes naught but from itself. Love possesses not nor would it be possessed; for love is sufficient unto love. When you love you should not say, "God is in my heart," but rather, I am in the heart of God." And think not you can direct the course of love, if it finds you worthy, directs your course. Love has no other desire but to fulfill itself. But if you love and must needs have desires, let these be your desires: To melt and be like a running brook that sings its melody to the night. To know the pain of too much tenderness: To be wounded by your own understanding of love; And to bleed willingly and joyfully. To wake at dawn with a winged heart and give thanks for another day of loving; To rest at the noon hour and meditate love's ecstasy; To return home at eventide with gratitude; And then to sleep with a prayer for the beloved in your heart and a song of praise upon your lips. Khalil Gibran

"Begin All Thinking, and Action with the Name of the Heavenly Father, the Holy Mother, the Divine Son, and the Holy Spirit"

The Kemetic Holistic Life Coaching Training Program is a counseling program under the Lion of Judah Ministries

Question: What is a Kemetic Holistic Life Coach?

Answer: A Kemetic Holistic Life Coach helps people in various areas of life find MAAT **(balance, order, harmony,)** using ancient sacred Kemetic (Egyptian) principles. It is a type of counseling that can be used to help people who are in **major transition phases** in their lives. Kemetic Life Coaches often try to help people plan goals and take steps to realize those goals. The KHLC first, teaches the Kemetic Sacred Way of Life, and second, offers advice and guidance to deal with change that will put the client on a path to success.

Question: What does **holistic** refer to in the title Kemetic Holistic Life Coach?

Answer: Holistic is really a triune approach, or a mind, body, spirit approach, instead of approaching a problem as a separate component. The Kemetic Holistic Life Coach is **"holistic"** in his/her approach, and knows that **"everything is connected"**.

He/she is also all about getting to the **root cause** of an issue, not just looking at the **symptoms or effect**, but seeks out the **cause** of the situation, and effectively treats the symptoms. The Kemetic Holistic Life Coach will get to the root cause of whatever is troubling the client, whether it is stress related, or an addiction problem. He/she will investigate every area of the client's life (holistically) to determine the root cause of the problem.

Question: What are some reasons a person would need a Kemetic Holistic Life Coach?

Answer: There might be a number of reasons why a person might seek the guidance of a Kemetic Holistic Life Coach. For instance, they might feel stagnant in their life and need advice on how to move forward. Others, however, seek the guidance of life coaches for help at different turning points in their lives, such as:

Finishing their education

Starting a career

Starting a new career

Advancing a career

Moving on from divorce

Buying a home

Reorganizing financial goals

Becoming free of Addictions

Learning and applying "Holistic Health"

Personal goals such as spiritual and cultural development

There are certain traits and skills that an individual should possess in order to succeed in a Kemetic Holistic Life Coaching career. Kemetic Life Coaches should live a Kemetic Sacred Life, **(live and apply what they teach)** be energetic, inspirational, motivational, and organizational. Excellent listening and communication skills are also a must. The Kemetic Holistic Life Coach should be knowledgeable in a variety of areas, and current events.

Question: What does a KHLC do when they first meet a client?

Answer: Before a Kemetic Holistic Life Coach can help a client, she/he first needs to initiate an in depth interview. During this interview, the coach should be made aware of what a client's wants, needs, and goals are in life. Kemetic Holistic Life Coaches offer guidance to all types of people in different stages of their lives. Some Kemetic Holistic Life Coaches might focus solely on certain types of situations, like advancing careers, while others may be willing to help with life transition. A good coach will often act as a sounding board for his/her clients. He/she is often expected to listen closely to their concerns and problems. The coach should be able to look at a client's life with an unbiased eye and offer fresh perspectives on certain situations. In doing so, the coach will usually be able to help his/her client work through any problems he/she may face.

Question: Should a Kemetic Holistic Life Coach take the same approach with each client?

Answer: Good question: And the answer is NO! Helping each client should be specialized and different for everyone; it is a very individualized process. Methods that work for one client, for instance, may not work for another. Because of this, a good coach will develop plans based on each client's strengths,

weaknesses, abilities, and limitations. A life coach will also usually take into consideration each client's morals and values.

Another important duty of a Kemetic Holistic Life Coach is to keep track of his clients' progress. He/she will often give them action-oriented homework assignments that are designed to help them move toward their goals, for instance. A good coach also often demands accountability from his clients, but also acts as a source of inspiration and encouragement.

*NOTE – Check the laws and Insurance requirements for Life Coaching in your state.

Question: Have you ever worked as a Life Coach?

Answer: I have worked as a Mental Health Counselor for many years, and I have helped many individuals, families, and students solve their problems and find treatment when needed. This is why I developed The Kemetic Holistic Life Coaching Program. I wanted to use my years of experience as a Mental Health Counselor, and my knowledge of Ancient Kemetic Principles to teach people how to live a happy, and fulfilling, sacred life.

THE KEMETIC SACRED LIFE

Question: What is the Kemetic Sacred Life?

Answer: The Kemetic Sacred Life is a return to the appreciation for family, friends, community, country, nature, being ethical, respecting all people, having high moral values, developing spirituality, having value for human life, and love for the creator.

KEMETIC SACRED PRINCIPLES

EVERYTHING STARTS WITH SPIRIT

Question: Who is Amen?

Answer: Amen means hidden, Amen represents the hidden force underlying creation. Amen represents the SPIRIT that animates the universe and all its components (attributes) and creation. When Amen is joined with RA (Amen-Ra) the force represents the animated power of creation. This is the same concept taken out of ancient Kemet and used by the Hebrews as YHWH (HUHI) and ELOHEEM. YHWH ELOHEEM is the **Creative Force of Will/ Eternal Creator.**

AMEN MANIFESTED THE **I AM, THE SPIRIT THAT CREATES AND ANIMATES** THE HUMAN BODY WHILE WE ARE LIVING, THIS IS THE "CHRIST" OR THE "BREATH OF LIFE" **"RUACH HAKADOSH"**

- **Note Amen is given praise at the end of every Judaic, Christian, and Islamic prayer.**

Question: Who is Amen in the Scriptures?

Answer: First, we have to go to the book of Revelations 3:14, and remember this is in red letters, so as we know red letters refer to "Christ". **Christ is the "hidden one" in us,** Christ is **THE AMEN. Christ is the Faithful and True Witness: {Red letter} 14** "And to the angel of the church of the Laodiceans [a] write, '**these things say the Amen, the Faithful and True Witness, the Beginning of the creation of God:** Here the definite article "THE" is being used to denote "A noun- a being". **"These things say the Amen"**

The **Creator, Witness, and Original Creation** is explained in John 1: that all existence is spiritual, that it comes to man as a gift, and that Christ is its fulfillment. "In the beginning was the Word, and the Word was with God (Amen), and the Word was (Amen) God."

Question: What is the WORD?

Answer: The WORD is the **divine idea (The Son)**--the Christ or Word of God, and God is Omnipresent.

2 The same was in the beginning with God. **(This ties into Revelation 3:14 Amen, the Faithful and True Witness, the Beginning of the creation of God) This "WORD" is the witness of the Creation of GOD, the first Creation is "Mental", and this is the "only begotten God". (*note Son of God was not in the original text) The second creation is created by YHWH –OF THE ELOHEEM,**

This Creation is the manifestation of the mental creation by Divine Mind. Here YHWH ELOHEEM (Eternal Creator) brings things (thoughts ideas into the material or objective realm.

3All things were made by him; and without him was not anything made that was made. 4In him was life; and the life was the light of men. 5 And the light shines in darkness; and the darkness comprehended it not.

SPIRITUAL STIMULANTS

John 3 Iu'sus Karast – Jesus Christ answered and said unto him, Verily, verily, I say unto thee, except a man be born again, he cannot see the kingdom of God. *Jesus*

John 4:13, 14 Iu'sus Karast – Jesus Christ answered and said unto her, Whosoever drinketh of this water shall thirst again:

But whosoever drinketh of the water that I shall give him shall never thirst; but the water that I shall give him shall be in him a well of water springing up into everlasting life. *Jesus*

Health is the greatest gift, contentment the greatest wealth, faithfulness the best relationship. *Buddha*

Our greatest glory is not in ever falling, but in getting up every time we do. *Confucius*

Forgiveness: Thus saith the Lord, "Verily those who are patient in adversity and forgive wrongs are the doers of excellence." *Muhammad*

Maat – Law of balance, order, harmony and peace

Question: What is Maat (Mayet)?

Answer: Ma-at represents the principle of Kosmic order; the concept by which not only Human Beings, but also Neteru (Gods/Eloheem/Angelic Beings) themselves are governed. **Ma-at signifies balance, harmony, order, peace, tranquility, and equilibrium** between all the Kosmic Forces of nature (Neteru).

Ma-at is usually portrayed as a woman wearing a headdress with an ostrich feather attached. Ma-at represents the abstract concept of order, justice, truth, righteousness, and "What is right", in all their purest forms. Ma-at is the ideal of balance: of things working as they should work. Without Ma-at chaos reigns unchecked, and the ability to create order is forever lost. That is to say, Ma-at is order on its most abstract level: that which causes everything to exist and continues to exist.

Question: What does Ma-at mean in human terms?

Answer: In human terms, Ma-at represents **"The Right Thing to Do All of The Time"**. Our Kemetic Ancestors perceived the universe in terms of dualism between Ma-at: **Truth and Order** vs **Disorder and Chaos:** Ma-at as shown below is usually portrayed in the double form of Ma-at.

Ma-at represents the law of creation. In order to create the dynamics necessary for progression and extension from the unity, an Asymmetrical division is needed. Our Ancient Kemetic

Ancestor's representation of 1/2 (shown below) clearly shows sides of un-equal length, this indicates Asymmetrical division.

The glyph for Ma-at is the same as the glyph for 1/2, showing that Ma-at represents the law of Asymmetric division. As the model for Cosmic harmony, order, balance, and equilibrium, Ma-at is associated with many functions, such as: 1. The administration of justice. All high ranking Ancient Kemet were described as priests of Ma-at, and the chief justice wore a little figure of Ma-at around his neck, as a badge of the office.

Ma-at is sometimes represented "having her eyes closed" to ensure equal justice for all. Ma-at in her double form represents the two opposing sides of a litigation, because the scale of justice cannot balance without the equality of the opposing forces. In the Hall of Judgment, Ma-at is depicted in double form. The forty-two Assessors are under Ma-at's charge.

All the activities of the Kemetic Sacred Life, including building temples, were devoted to the maintenance of Ma-at. The temple's rituals were based upon and coordinated with the movements of the heavens, which were in turn manifestations of the divine cosmic law.

Ma-at is maintained in the world by the correct actions (Tehuti), and personal piety in truth. The ultimate objective of the earthly man is to develop his/her consciousness to the utmost perfection; it means that he/she becomes harmoniously tuned with nature. On Judgment Day, the successful person is declared to be sound and pure by the grand Jury (The 42 Assessors/Neteru). (The True Voice)

Ma-at is related to the societal orderly relationship and harmony. Ma-at is related to the harmonic laws of music. (Harmonic Vibrations)

Ma-at and Seshat are the counterparts to Tehuti

BUILDING THE TEMPLE

WHAT IS SPIRIT AND SOUL?

THE SPIRIT AND SOUL

Question: What Is A Soul?

Answer: The soul is man's consciousness; it is the underlying idea behind any expression. In man, the soul is the many accumulated ideas behind his present expression. In its original and true sense, the soul of man is the expressed idea of man in Divine Mind.

The soul is the self, the "I" that inhabits the body and acts through it. Without the soul, the body is like a light bulb without electricity, a computer without the software, a space suit with no astronaut inside. With the introduction of the soul, the body acquires life, sight and hearing, thought and speech, intelligence and emotions, will and desire, personality and identity.

Symbols of the KA and the BA- the spirit and the soul

The human soul is both the most complex and the loftiest of souls. There are five names for the soul in Hebrew: Nefesh (soul), Ruach (spirit), Neshamah (breath), Chayah (life) and Yechidah. The soul's five "names" actually describe five levels or dimensions of the soul. Nefesh is the soul as the engine of physical life. Ruach is the emotional self and "personality." Neshamah is the intellectual self. Chayah is the supra-rational self--the seat of will, desire, commitment and faith. Yechidah is the essence of the soul--its unity with its source, the singular essence of Yahuwa. For the essence of the soul of man is "literally a part of Yahuwa in us.

Question: Are there two souls in the human being?

Answer: Yes, there are two distinct souls that are one, and vitalize the human being: an "Animal Soul" and a "Divine Soul or the "I AM." The Animal Soul is driven by the quest for self-preservation and self-enhancement; in this, it resembles the soul and self of all other creations. But we also possess a Divine Soul or "Huwa" in us"--a soul driven by the desire to reconnect with our Divine Source.

On a daily basis our lives are the story of a contest, as we strive on the battlefield between these two souls, as we struggle to balance and reconcile our physical needs and desires with our spiritual aspirations. These two souls, however, do not reside "side-by-side" within the body; rather, the Divine Soul is encased within the Animal Soul--just as the Animal Soul is encased within the body. This means that the Animal Soul, too, is vitalized by the "part of "Yahuwa-G-D" above" at its core. Even though the two souls are in conflict with each other, in essence they are compatible with each other.

Symbolic of the Dual Souls

Question: how has the word Soul been Mistranslated?

Answer: In the Holy Books: Torah, The Old Testament (Genesis 17:14), New Testament (Matthew 12:18) As Well As The Noble Koran (The Noble Koran 4:171), You Will See That scholars Mistranslate And Misuse The Word 'Soul' in every sect of religion. The Soul Or Spirit Is Not Some Ghost Like Apparition Or Some Spiritual Being Like Paintings, Pictures, or Statues.

An example of how the word 'soul' has been mistranslated can be found in genesis 1:2 and i quote: bible – Old Testament, genesis 1:2'and the earth was without form, and void; and darkness was upon the face of the deep. And the spirit of god moved upon the face of the waters.'

King James Version of the bible

Take a look at the Hebrew word **ruwach   meaning, wind, breath, and mind.** Also in the Koran 70:4, where it states and I Quote: The Koran 70:4

Whereby, the entire heavenly host and the soul **(Jesus Christ)** shall elevate unto him in a day whose length is fifty thousand years.

Translated by:

Faheem Judah-El D.D.

In Arabic, the word ruwh   is used meaning, breath of life, soul. Now, this is how the confusion starts. Why would they translate the word rooakh   in Hebrew or ruwh   in Arabic as spirit when in actuality the word spirit is Nafs   in Arabic and Nefesh   in Hebrew? Either it was deliberately done or the people who translated it do not know the language nor do they know that there is a difference between spirit and soul themselves.

Spirit Ka = nafs or nefesh

Soul Ba= ruwh or rooakh

Clarke's Bible Commentary explains the exact point I'm making here. In genesis 1:24 it states, and i quote: 'and God said, let the earth bring forth the living creature after his kind…'

'Let the earth bring forth the living creature   nephesh hayyum; a general term to express all creatures endued with animal life.'

Clarke's bible commentary, volume 1, Genesis – Deuteronomy

Now in this verse it says 'living creature' and translates as nefesh hayyum in Hebrew. Here Clarke is uncertain of the correct definition of nefesh / spirit and ruwach / soul. Yet, in Genesis 1:2 as previously stated, he translates 'Spirit of God', based on the Hebrew word ruwach, which should be translated as "nefesh".

"The Spirit of God": this phrase has been misunderstood by many scholars. Some think it refers to a violent wind because ruach often signifies wind, as well as spirit, as pneuma does in the Greek.'

Clarke's Bible Commentary, Volume I, Genesis – Deuteronomy

Also lane Arabic – English lexicon defines ruwh as: the soul, spirit, or vital principal; syn. ; (but there is a difference between these two words, for they are not always interchangeable...).

However, the Greek translation shows the following definitions of spirit and soul: Psuch soul. Life mind; the breath of life; the vital force which animates the body and shows itself in breathing which can be found in mark 8:36.

Bible – New Testament Mark 8:36 (With Greek Inserts)

For What Shall It Profit A Man, If He Shall Gain The Whole World, And Lose His Own Soul?

King James Version of The Bible

Pneuma: Spirit; A Movement Of Air (A Gentle Blast); The Spirit, The Vital Principal By Which The Body Is Animated; The Rational Spirit Which Can Be Found In Matthew 3:16.

Bible – New Testament Matthew 3:16

And Jesus, when he was baptized, went up straightway out of the water; and, lo, the heavens were opened unto him, and he saw the spirit of god descending like a dove, and lighting upon him:

King James Version of the Bible

So, the problem of overstanding the difference between spirit and soul is not from the person reading the scriptures, it stems from the translator. Your religious leaders are at fault because they don't know any other languages and therefore have to rely on these mistranslations. Even if what they read doesn't make sense to them they will relay it to hundreds of thousands of their followers believing without a doubt that this translated scripture is correct.

Let's Further Examine The Word Ruwh   In Arabic from the Root Raaha, Which Means: 'It was violently windy'. Al Ruwhul Quwdus means The Holy Soul. You can see how one meaning can be physical and the other is spiritual in meaning.

In Hebrew the root of ruwach means, 'to blow, breathe.'

Ruwach = mind, spirit, wind.

Ruwach – Wind- Physical, by resemblance breath, a sensible (or even violent) exhalation; life, anger, insubstantiality; a region in the sky; by resemblance spirit, but only of a rational being (its expression and functions): air, anger, blast, breath, cool, courage, mind, quarter, side, spirit, tempest, vain (whirl wind).

Ezekiel 1:12 each one went straight ahead. Wherever the spirit would go, they would go, without turning as they went.

In the Book of Ezekiel, in his vision: The spirit that took him up is the wind from a ship, the Mother ship. It is called the holy city in Revelation 21:2 as the 'New Jerusalem'.

Question: Was Ezekiel's vision real or abstract?

Answer: This vision was abstract, so it has to be broken down by the symbols in the vision.

Question: What do you mean?

Answer: Let's take the meaning of "Ruwach or wind" in this vision, the scene in the vision is physical, and it has physical symbols such as wind, but this wind is only a symbol with a spiritual meaning.

Question: Can you give us an example?

Answer: Yes, let's take the word "Ruwach or wind", wind is a spiritual symbol of life currents that come from within and surround the whole being; the executive power of mind clearing the way to higher states of consciousness.

Question: What do cities mean in the Bible?

Answer: Cities are symbols of fixed states of consciousness in the various nerve centers of the body. The presiding or central thought-meaning of a city is found in the significance of its name, combined with that of the man, tribe, country, or nation with which it is mentioned.

In their highest significance, the "cities of Judah" (II Sam. 2:1) represent spiritual centers of life in consciousness.

"The city which has the foundations whose builder and maker is God" (Heb. 11:10) is the spiritual body. Its foundation is the ideal body created by Divine Mind. By faith we bring this ideal body into manifestation.

So from the city (fixed state of consciousness, to naming that city such as Judah – Judah represents the ganglionic center at the very apex of the brain that we may term the center of reverence

or spirituality. It is there that man holds converse with the intelligence of Divine Mind. This brain center is the home or "house" of a spiritual consciousness, which is in Scripture designated as Judah, whose office it is to pray and praise. This faculty is also called the super-consciousness; that is, it is above the various states of mind, but not separate from them. It pervades every phase of thought as an elevating, inspiring quality. Jesus Christ (Iye-su Karast) is from the Tribe of Judah.

Explained by Faheem Judah-El D.D.

And I John saw the holy city, New Jerusalem (the faculty of a new consciousness based on spiritual peace), coming down from God (Divine Mind) out of heaven (The realm of Divine Mind; a state of consciousness in harmony with the thoughts of Divine Mind. prepared as a bride adorned for her husband. (A union of two states of consciousness)

In this quote Revelation 21:2, the word they translated as 'heaven' from Greek is 'Ouranos' which is the Greek word for 'Orion'.

Question: So is the translation of Heaven as a place like Orion correct?

Answer: First let me say the message God Most High sends us is spiritual, we know this physical state of consciousness is

temporary, so to go to a place like Orion or the Moon in a physical state is not the message God Most High is sending us. Heaven is the realm of Divine Mind; a state of consciousness in harmony with the thoughts of the Most High. Heaven is everywhere present. It is "Maat" the orderly, lawful adjustment of The Most High's kingdom in man's mind, body, and affairs.

Question: Is heaven a place in our solar system?

Answer: No, these places are symbolic in the scriptures, but Our Teacher, Lord, and Savior Iu-em-Hetep (Jesus Christ) gave heaven a definite location. He said, **"The kingdom of Yahweh (Yahuwa) is within you" (Luke 17:21). Heaven is within every one of us; a place, a conscious sphere of mind, having all the attraction described or imagined as belonging to heaven.** But this kingdom within is not material, it is spiritual. I'm not saying beings were not able to go from planet to planet, but that is not the spiritual message we need to help us build the great temple.

Question: Is the spirit what takes you to the next plane?

Answer: Yes, it is the state of the spirit that determines whether you move to a higher plane, this can happen if one has burnt out the desire for the physical plane. The person who has strong love for the physical world will desire rebirth into the physical plane. You must negate this world to move on to the next life. The spirit fights the urges of physical desires that stem from emotions.

Bible – New Testament 1 John 2:15

Love Not The World, Neither The Things That Are In The World. If Any Man Love The World, The Love Of The Father Is Not In Him.

King James Version of the Bible

Question: How are emotions related with physical desires?

Answer: Our Great Teacher, Lord and Savior taught us that desires stem from emotions. For example you have: 1. Sexual emotions, which is the desire for pleasure. 2. Then you have the gluttonous emotions, which is the desire for an extreme amount of food. 3. And you have greed emotions, which is the desire for everything whether you need it or not. And when you don't get these things, it sets these emotions into motion. These are the emotions that if you don't get what you want, makes you angry, make you fight, or even makes you kill. Anger is the most devastating emotion.

For example:

Gluttony

Gluttony causes overeating, which leads to obesity which leads to sickness and disease, which can lead to death.

Lust

Uncontrolled Sexual desires leads to lust which can lead to sexually transmitted diseases which can lead to HIV-AIDS and eventually death. Don't let sexual desires let you take chances you wouldn't normally take and regret them once you have aids. It is important to be in control of your emotions.

Anger

It is important to control anger. Many people die un-necessarily because they can't control their anger. Don't let your inability to control anger get you into trouble because you can't control your tongue. Don't put yourself in a position where you have killed someone or you're in a situation where you are about to be killed because you can't control your anger. "When two people are sitting down and start arguing, one or both will stand up, at this point the anger is about to become motion and action. Just sit down and the energy will calm down."

Question: Why is anger the most devastating emotion?

Answer: Because anger is the most un-controllable emotion, and it is the greatest enemy of peace, for it is the most negative, and it can instantly cause the most permanent damage.

Anger does great danger to the mind and the body as well. The whole nervous system is damaged by one fit of anger.

There are times when a spiritual teacher expresses a little anger outwardly in order to correct a student. However, this should not be confused with un-controlled emotional anger. The Teacher may appear to be angry, but the true master remains cool within, for his or her motive is the growth of his or her disciples. Only when anger is the outcome of selfish or petty motives is it wrong. Anger is very difficult to control and especially when it has been allowed to fester and become habitual. It can be controlled when it is a small ripple in the subconscious mind. Watch the mind carefully for any signs of irritability; frequent irritation can be a sign of mental weakness. One has to be able to let go of the small things in life, and develop the virtue of patience in one's life. Just as heat and light can be transferred into electricity, anger can be transferred into spiritual energies.

1. The Crown Chakra

2. The Third Eye Chakra

3. The Throat Chakra

4. The Heart Chakra

5. The Solar Plexus Chakra

6. The Sacral Chakra

7. The Base/Root Chakra

Question: What is meant by the spiritual plane?

Answer: First, we must ask what is a plane? There are many planes of life, one above or below another, yet not conflicting. All creation is based on life activity, or as it is called in physical science, rates of vibration. A certain activity in the life current forms worlds on a plane, which we may call the physical; a little increase in the vibratory rate makes another system, which we may designate as the psychical; a still higher rate makes a universe where spiritual ideas prevail. These are all interlaced and interblended in the presence around and within us, hence the **"kingdom of God is within you" (Luke 17:21),** or "among you," as one translator gives it.

There is the spiritual plane also called the astral plane as well as other planes, but the most common mistake is imagining planes as layers lying one above the other in space. This is incorrect. As I have said many times, everything is vibration, which manifests itself in different moods and schemes. Planes are the different realms of ideas in which men function.

The best way to express vibration is called mood. So planes are moods and schemes of vibrations existing in very unique and unified forms and may be liken to varying degrees of temperature such as extremely low, to extremely high.

The natural mood of vibration ranges from very high and fast to very low and slow and are distinct and intricate moods of vibration woven into one another so uniquely that one cannot determine where one plane begins and the other ends.

VIBRATIONS

Question: Can you explain more about what vibrations are?

Answer: Vibrations are the rate at which all forces move. One of the greatest discoveries of all ages is that of physical science which shows that all things have their source and being in vibrations. What Lord Jesus (Iu-Em-Hetep) taught so profoundly in symbols about the riches of the kingdom of the heavens has now been proved true.

The whole universe is in vibration, and that vibration is under law (Maat). Chaos would result if the law were not supreme. Each particular thing has its rate of vibration. Heat, light, and color are different rates of vibration in one field of primal energy. Different colors are caused by the different frequencies of the vibrations as they strike the eye. But what causes vibration?

Question: What causes vibration?

Answer: Mind. Vibrations, thoughts – energies sent out by force and power of thought.

Nothing in existence rests. Every sense man has vibrates and everything you see, hear or touch vibrates. Vibration is what keeps the universe in order. The soul is what enables man to tune into these vibrations of the universe.

Man vibrates on the alpha wave length. It is the middle c note in music. This note causes vibration within the chemistry of the body itself. There are seven planes (just as there are seven notes in music) and each plane has its purpose as all things have their purpose, just as you have a purpose for being here.

Advanced Mental

Lahuwt Heavenly Abode

Ether Body   Ether Soul

7 Bosom   1 Eternal Bliss

6 Divine Reality 2 Spark of life

5 Divine Truth   3 Guardian Angels

The Fourth Plane Is Where Man And Mind Meet And They Balance Everything.

Malakuwt Angelic Abode

4 Mental Plane   4 Spirit/Soul = 8 ogdad

Thoughts Are FORMED

3 Spiritual Plane   5 Emotions Are Manifest

2 Plane Of Force   6 The Force between voluntary and Involuntary Actions which Is Life's Substance

---

Naasuwt - Physical Abode

1 Material Plane   7 Carnal Desire

Spirit   Body Material

Submerge Mental

The Seven Planes Have Seven Sub – Planes That You Are Able To See By The Seven Sub Planes Of The Material Plane

Question: was it possible for Jesus (Iu-em-Hetep) to visualize the lowest sub – planes?

Answer: Yes, in Ephesians 4:9–10 we read, - 9 (Now this, "He ascended"—what does it mean but that He also first descended into the lower parts of the earth? 10 He who descended is also the One who ascended far above all the heavens, that He might fill all things.)

In order to visualize the lower sub – planes of the spiritual world, Jesus (Iu-em-Hetep) had to maintain a positive mental state which would allow Him to act as a barrier through which the negative influences cannot penetrate.

His first impression would have been that the material world was still around Him with all its scenery plainly visible. As He looked, He would have found a peculiar veil between those scenes and the plane upon which He temporarily dwelled. This veil, though transparent, seems to have a peculiar appearance of resistant solidity as He realized that it was a barrier to the passage into the mental plane.

Jesus would have changed his Vibrations to witness a very unpleasant Sub-Plane called the **'Spiritual Chemistry'**. This Sub-Plane would have been full of ghastly appearances of its

surroundings. From all sides He would have seen disintegrating forms of human beings and animals that seem to float in space, seeming real, yet somewhat unreal. These disintegrating spiritual forms are 'spiritual shells'. Just as the physical body has a corpse, so does the spiritual body, and moves on to higher planes of the spiritual beings. The shell is left until it disintegrates and disappears.

Question: How long does the spiritual shell remain on the lower Sub-level plane?

Answer: Not all spiritual shells remain on the sub planes, but the time an individual 'spiritual shell' remains on this plane depends on the spiritual desires of the person, and if they have a good heart. With good ideals the soul will fade away into the higher realm very rapidly; its atoms having little or no cohesive attraction to the lower physical world.

Question: What would happen to a person who has great love for the physical world?

Answer: As I was about to say, But, on the other hand, the spiritual shell of the individual with love and desire for the physical world and all it offers will hold together a long time and be bound to this plane. These spiritual shells are held together a long time. They are dead and have no consciousness or intelligence, unlike 'specters' or 'shades'.

Question: Are there only evil or material beings on the sub-plane?

Answer, No these are planes of elevation for some, and on this particular plane Jesus (Iu-em-Hetep) would have felt the presence of great spiritual entities, which guarded this plane. They were Etherians who protect the slumber of the souls that rest therein. He would have seen slight movements indicating the awakening of some of the resting forms; a moment, and the forms would disappear. The vibrations would change and the soul moved to another sub-plane to begin its real life after death.

All souls, however high or low, eventually move off the spiritual and enter into the state of the mental plane; or regain in the heavens whoever they leave behind, their spiritual shells on the heavens (planes). The souls spend much time enjoying the well-earned bliss.

Souls lower in development spend less time in the higher regions because of their love for the world. These spiritual forms are most repulsive and almost beastlike in appearance, rather than human. There are still lower forms on the sub-divisions below. The 'creatures' sojourning therein are sub-spiritual bodies awakened from their brief spiritual sleep to find themselves in what you call 'hell'.

Question: what and where is hell?

Answer: "The English word hell is from the Saxon verb helan, 'to cover, or conceal,' and intrinsically contains no idea of a place of torment, and never did smell of fire and brimstone in its Saxon home."

One does not have to die in order to go to hell, any more than one has to die to go to heaven. Both are states of mind, and conditions, which people experience as a direct outworking of their thoughts, beliefs, words, and acts. If one's mental processes are out of harmony with the law of man's being, they result in trouble and sorrow; mental as well as bodily anguish overtakes one, and this is hell. If this remains the state of a being until physical death, the person stays in a state of hell because of attachment to physical or material mind.... worldly thoughts, ideas, desires.

The material world is seen as a background. It appears as a movie green screen, but to the souls in a state of hell whom have experienced physical death, only the lowest of earthly activity can be seen. The higher spiritual activities are blotted out to them. To these souls there is no earth except these scenes, which are filled with their own desires. Desires that only lead to suffering. This is hell for them for they cannot participate. They can exercise only the **'lust of the eye'**. These departed souls see their friends eating, drinking, gambling, fornicating, and

engaging in all forms of violence and brutality. Meanwhile, as they eagerly cluster around these scenes they cannot participate. Their lack of a physical body is a barrier to their ungodliness.

The souls in hell **(a state of mind)** may be able to find an old earthly companion saturated with liquor, shooting drugs and unlawful sex. Their mindless desire for physical ecstasy continues to grow with each memorable occurrence. However, in due time, the desire reaches a climax and starts to reverse; and with the reversal comes revitalization of the soul to a 'rebirth'.

The soul that once was opened to evil influences and desires has now been given a chance to rise up the spiritual scale. This is the burning out of desire for the world. Even the lowest of souls rise in time. In these hells of the spiritual, the degraded souls are punished not for their sins, but by their sins.

In the majority of cases, the dying person sinks into the slumber of death and awakens after a period of restful transformation. In some cases, however, there is a brief awakening like a semi-awakening from a dream shortly after departure from the spiritual body. In this instance, the spiritual body may appear visible to a friend or loved one. The spirit soon becomes drowsy and sinks into the preliminary sleep of the spiritual plane.

Now I have a question for you, who is the Savior, and redeemer of these beings, and the entire world?

Matthew 5:45

So that you will become children of your Father in heaven, because he makes his sun rise on both evil and good people, and he lets rain fall on the righteous and the unrighteous.

The Sons of Sananda, and the Children of the Most High need little preparation to move on to higher spiritual planes, when they leave the sukkot, tabernacle or physical body they may slumber only a very short period of time. If they believe that Iu-em-Hetep, Yeshua Ha Mashiakh, Jesus Christ is the Word, and the Word was with Yahuwa-God, and the Word was God. 2 He was with Yahuwa-God in the beginning. 3 Through him all things were made; without him nothing was made that has been made. 4 In him was life, and that life was the light of all mankind. 5 The light shines in the darkness, and the darkness has not overcome[a] it. 9 The true light that gives light to everyone was coming into the world. 10 He was in the world, and though the world was made through him, the world did not recognize him. 11 He came to that which was his own, but his own did not receive him. 12 Yet to all who did receive him, to those who believed in his name, he gave the right to become children of Yahuwa-God— 13 children born not of natural

descent, nor of human decision or a husband's will, but born of Yahuwa-God.14 The Word became flesh and made his dwelling among us. We have seen his glory, the glory of the one and only Son, who came from the Father, full of grace and truth. 15 (John testified concerning him. He cried out, saying, "This is the one I spoke about when I said, 'He who comes after me has surpassed me because he was before me.'") 16 Out of his fullness we have all received grace in place of grace already given. 17 For the law was given through Moses; grace and truth came through Jesus Christ. 18 No one has ever seen Yahuwa-God, but the one and only Son, who is himself Yahuwa-God and is in closest relationship with the Father, has made him known.

KEMETIC HOLISTIC LIFE COACHING KEYS

HU – SIA – HEKA
THE TRIAD OF THE MIND

Question: how do we bring more power **(Sekhem)** into our life?

Answer: People would love to get more power in the form of wealth, health, mind power (consciousness), but the fact is all we need to do is **live the spirit of these things** until they become ours by right. It will then become impossible to keep them from us. The things of the world are fluid to a power within us by which we inherently rule them.

Question: how do we acquire this power?

Answer: You don't have to acquire this power. You already have it. But you need to overstand it; you need to use it; you need to control it; you need to impregnate yourself with it, so that you can go forward and live your Sacred Life.

Every day, as you trod through creation, as you gain momentum, as your inspiration deepens, as your plans materialize, as you gain overstanding, you will come to realize that this world is not merely piles of trees and rocks, but that it is a living system! It is made up of the beating hearts of humanity. It is alive and beautiful. It is evident that it requires overstanding to work with

material of this description, but those who come into this overstanding are inspired by a new light, a new force, they gain confidence and greater power each day, they realize their hopes and dreams will come true. This new life, which is a **sacred life** has a richer, deeper, fuller, and clearer meaning than life before. This life is your original way of life; it is your **Sacred Kemetic Life.**

Question: are you saying we have to change how we see things in life?

Answer: I'm saying mind is **creative**, and it **conditions**. Our environment and all experiences in life are the result of our habitual or predominant mental attitude. Thoughts are like planets, they orbit in our minds, and if the thoughts are negative, they continuously go around and around keeping us in the same conditions mentally as well as physically.

Question: so we must change our attitude in life?

Answer: the attitude of mind depends upon what we think. Therefore, **the secret of all power, all achievement and all possession depends upon our method of thinking.**

We must "be" before we can "do" and we can "do" only to the extent that we "are," and what we "are" depends upon what we "think."

We cannot express powers that we do not possess. The only way by which we may secure possession of power is to become conscious of power, and we can never become conscious of power until we learn that all power is from within. There is a world within—a world of thought and feeling and power; of light and life and beauty, and although invisible, its forces are mighty.

SPIRITUAL STIMULANT

John 1

1 In the beginning was the Word, and the Word was with God, and the Word was God. 2 He was in the beginning with God. 3 All things were made through Him, and without Him nothing was made that were made. **4 In Him was life, and the life was the light of men.**

The world within is governed by mind (SIA). When we discover this world we shall find the solution for every problem, the cause for every effect; and since the world within is subject to our control, all laws, of power and possession is also within our control.

The world without is a reflection of the world within. What appears without is what has been found within. In the world within may be found **infinite Wisdom, infinite Power, infinite**

Supply of all that is necessary, waiting for **unfoldment, development and expression.** If we recognize these potentialities in the world within they will take form within the world without.

MAAT – HARMONY

Question: I thought potentialities represented (Nun) or Chaos within?

Answer: In the world within potentialities or Nun are brought into order, peace, balance and harmony by Maat. Harmony in the world within is reflected in the world without by harmonious conditions, agreeable surroundings, and the best of everything. It is the foundation of health, and a necessary essential to all greatness, all power, all attainment, all achievement and all success.

Question: how do we achieve harmony within?

Answer: We achieve harmony within by the ability to control our thoughts, emotion, desires, and to determine for ourselves how any experience is to affect us. We must master our animal consciousness, and lead with our "higher-God" consciousness. When we have harmony in the world within it results in optimism and affluence; so affluence within results in affluence without." The world without reflects the circumstances and the conditions of the consciousness within.

WISDOM

Question: what do you mean by the world within?

Answer: If we find wisdom in the world within, we shall have the overstanding to discern the wonderful possibilities that are latent in it, and we shall be given the power to make these possibilities manifest in the world without.

The world within is the practical world in which the men and women of power generate courage, hope, enthusiasm, confidence, trust and faith, by which they are given the divine intelligence to see the vision and the practical skill to make the vision real.

Question: what is life?

Answer: life is an enfoldment, not accretion. What comes to us in the world without is what we already possess in the world within.

Question: are the things we possess based on are thoughts?

Answer: all possession is based on consciousness. All gain is the result of an accumulative consciousness. All loss is the result of a scattering consciousness. Mental efficiency is contingent upon harmony; discord means confusion; therefore, if we want to acquire power we must be in harmony with Natural Law.

We are related to the world without by the **objective mind**. The brain is the organ of this mind, and the cerebro-spinal system of nerves puts us in conscious communication with every part of the body. This system of nerves responds to every sensation of light, heat, odor, sound and taste.

When this mind thinks correctly, when it overstands the truth, when the thoughts sent through the cerebro-spinal nervous

system to the body are constructive, and these sensations are pleasant, and harmonious. The result is that we build strength, vitality and all constructive forces into our body, but it is through this same objective mind that all distress, sickness, limitations and every form of discord and chaos is admitted to our lives. It is therefore through the objective mind, by wrong thinking, that we are related to all destructive forces.

Question: is the objective mind related to the world within?

Answer: no, we are related to the world within by the subconscious mind. The solar plexus is the organ of this mind; the sympathetic system of nerves presides over all subjective sensations, such as joy, fear, love, emotion, respiration, imagination and all other subconscious phenomena. It is through the subconscious that we are connected with the **Universal Mind** and brought into relation with the Infinite constructive forces of the Universe. (Neteru)

It is the co-ordination of these two centers of our being, and the overstanding of their functions, which is the great secret of life. With this knowledge we can bring the **objective and subjective minds** into conscious co-operation and thus co-ordinate the finite and the infinite. Our future is entirely within our own control.

Question: what is universal mind?

Answer: **UNIVERSAL MIND** is the source or life principle of every atom in existence.

THE UNIVERSAL LAW

Question: what is universal law?

Answer: your life is governed by law, by principles that never vary. Law is in operation at all times; in all places. Fixed laws underlie all human actions. For this reason, men who control giant industries are enabled to determine with absolute precision just what percentage of every hundred thousand people will respond to any given set of conditions.

It is well, however, to remember that while every effect is the result of a cause, the effect in turn becomes a cause, which creates other effects, which in turn create still other causes; so that when you put the law of attraction into operation you must remember that you are starting a train of causation for good or otherwise which may have endless possibilities.

We frequently hear it said, "A very distressing situation came into my life, which could not have been the result of my thought, as I certainly never entertained any thought which could have

such a result." We fail to remember that like attracts like in the mental world, and that the thought which we entertain brings to us certain friendships, companionships of a particular kind, and these in turn bring about conditions and environment, which in turn are responsible for the conditions of which we complain.

Question: does this have anything to do with the law of attraction?

Answer: yes, it is the combination of **Thought and Love** which forms the irresistible force, called the law of attraction. All natural laws are irresistible, the law of Gravitation, or Electricity, or any other law operates with mathematical exactness.

Question: do the laws vary from one to another?

Answer: no, there is no variation; it is only the channel of distribution which may be imperfect. If a bridge falls, we do not attribute the collapse to any variation of the law of gravitation. If a light fails us, we do not conclude that the laws governing electricity cannot be depended upon, and if the law of attraction seems to be imperfectly demonstrated by an inexperienced or uninformed person, we are not to conclude that the greatest and most infallible law upon which the entire system of creation depends has been suspended. We should rather conclude that a little more understanding of the law is required, for the same

reason that a correct solution of a difficult problem in mathematics is not always readily and easily obtained.

Question: how do we develop better thought patterns in the future?

Answer: things are created in the mental or spiritual world before they appear in the outward act or event. By the simple process of governing our thought forces today, we help create the events which will come into our lives in the future, perhaps even to-morrow. Educated desire is the most potent means of bringing into action the law of attraction.

Don't forget we must also live a Kemetic Sacred life that means developing and exhibiting good moral character, and a sense of unity and community.

Question: should this information be taught to young people?

Answer: yes, the truth must be told to each generation and to every people in new and different terms. Our Great Master Teacher Iu'sus Karast- Jesus Christ taught—"Believe that ye receive and ye shall receive," or when Paul said—"Faith is the substance of things not seen," or when modern science says— "The law of attraction is that law by which thought correlates with its object," each statement, when subjected to analysis, is

found to contain exactly the same truth, the only difference being in the form of presentation.

Mark 11:24

King James Version (KJV)

24 Therefore I say unto you, what things so ever ye desire, when ye pray, believe that ye receive them, and ye shall have them.

THE CONSCIOUS AND THE SUB CONSCIOUS MINDS

Question: can you explain the function of the conscious mind versus the sub conscious mind?

Answer: first let me explain the necessary interaction of the conscious and subconscious mind a how they require a similar interaction between the corresponding systems of nerves. The cerebro-spinal system is the organ of the conscious mind, and the sympathetic is the organ of the subconscious. The cerebro-spinal is the channel through which we receive conscious perception from the physical senses, and exercise control over the movements of the body. This system of nerves has its center in the brain.

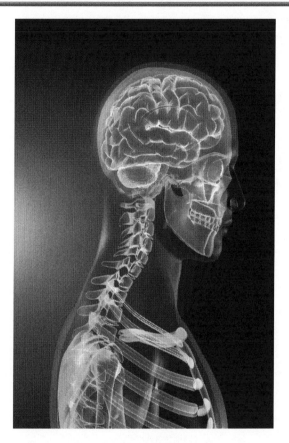

Cerebro-spinal system

The Sympathetic System has its center in a ganglionic mass at the back of the stomach known as the Solar Plexus, and is the channel of that mental action which unconsciously supports the vital functions of the body.

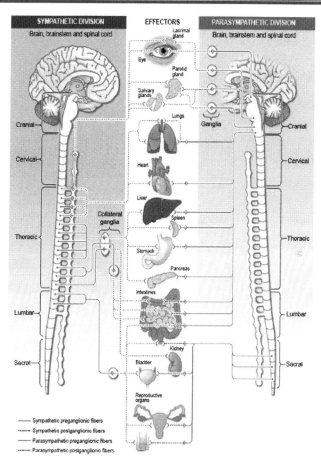

Solar Plexus Chakra Yang Pattern

Figure 2.3

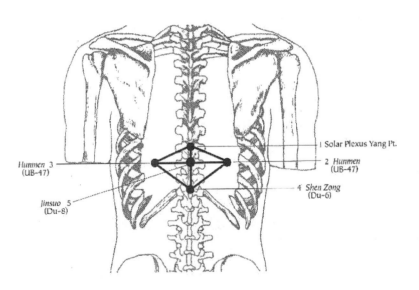

The connection between the two systems is made by the vagus nerve, which passes out of the cerebral region as a portion of the voluntary system to the thorax, sending out branches to the heart and lungs, and finally passing through the diaphragm it loses its outer coating and becomes identified with the nerves of the Sympathetic System, so forming a connecting link between the two and making man physically a single entity.

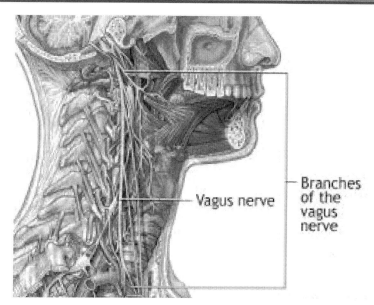

Vagus nerve

Branches of the vagus nerve

We have seen that every thought is received by the brain, which is the organ of the conscious; it is here subjected to our power of reasoning.

When the objective mind has been satisfied that the thought is true it is sent to the Solar Plexus, or the brain of the subjective mind, to be made into our flesh, to be brought into the world as a reality. It is then no longer susceptible to any argument whatever. The subconscious mind cannot argue; it only acts. It accepts the conclusions of the objective mind as final.

Question: why is it sent to the solar plexus?

Answer: because the Solar Plexus has been like the sun (Ra) of the body, because it is a central point of distribution for the energy which the body is constantly generating. This energy is very real energy, and this sun is a very real sun, the energy is being distributed by very real nerves to all parts of the body, and is thrown off in an atmosphere which envelops the body.

3 Solar plexus

If this radiation is sufficiently strong the person is called magnetic; he is said to be filled with personal magnetism. Such a person may wield an immense power for good. His presence alone will often bring comfort to the troubled minds with which he comes in contact.

Question: so you are saying if energy is been distributed properly through the solar plexus one should be healthy?

Answer: yes, when the Solar Plexus is in active operation and is radiating life, energy and vitality to every part of the body, and to everyone whom comes in contact with it, the sensations are pleasant; the body is filled with health and all with whom the person comes in contact experience a pleasant sensation.

Question: what happens to a person who is not getting the proper energy flow to the solar plexus?

Answer: If there is any interruption of this radiation the sensations are unpleasant, the flow of life and energy to some part of the body is stopped, and this is the cause of every illness to the human race, physical, mental or environmental.

Question: does this lack of energy flow affect us physically, or mentally?

Answer: physically because the sun of the body is no longer generating sufficient energy to vitalize some part of the body;

mentally because the conscious mind is dependent upon the subconscious mind for the vitality necessary to support its thought: and **environmentally** because the connection between the subconscious mind and the Universal mind is being interrupted.

The Solar Plexus is the point at which the part meets with the whole, where the finite becomes Infinite, where the **Uncreated** becomes **created,** the **Universal** becomes **individualized**, the **invisible** becomes **visible.** It is the point at which life appears, and there is no limit to the amount of life an individual may generate from this Solar center.

This center of energy is **Omnipotent** because it is the point of contact with all life and all intelligence. It can therefore accomplish whatever it is directed to accomplish, and here lies the power of the **conscious mind;** the **subconscious** can and will carry out such plans and ideas as may be suggested to it by the **conscious mind.**

Question: is conscious mind or subconscious mind the master of this center?

Answer: conscious thought is master of this sun center from which the **life and energy** (RA) of the entire body flows, and the quality of the thought which we entertain determines the quality of the thought which this sun will radiate, and the character of the thought which our conscious mind entertains will determine the character of the thought which this sun will radiate, and the nature of the thought which our conscious mind entertains will determine the nature of thought which this sun will radiate, and consequently will determine the nature of the experience which will result.

It is evident, therefore, that all we have to do is let our light shine; the more energy we can radiate, the more rapidly shall we be enabled to transmute undesirable conditions into sources of pleasure and profit.

Question: how do we let this light shine; how do we generate this energy.

Answer: through thought, or **non-resistant thought** which expands the Solar Plexus; **resistant thought contracts. Pleasant thought expands; unpleasant thought contracts.**

Question: what are the worst thought for the solar plexus?

Answer: thoughts of courage, power, confidence and hope all produce a corresponding state, but the one arch enemy of the Solar Plexus which must be absolutely destroyed before there is any possibility of letting any light shine is **fear.** This enemy must be completely destroyed; fear must be eliminated; fear must be expelled for ever; fear is the cloud which hides the sun; which causes a perpetual gloom.

Question: why is fear so bad for us?

Answer: fear is a kind of **kryptonite** which makes men fear the **past, the present and the future; fear themselves, their friends and their enemies; fear everything and everybody.** When fear is completely destroyed, your light will shine, the clouds will disperse and you will have found the source of power, energy and life.

When you find that you are really one with the Infinite power of ALL, and when you can consciously realize this power by a practical demonstration of your ability to overcome any adverse condition by the power of your thought, you will have nothing to fear; fear will have been destroyed and you will have come into possession of your true birthright.

Question: is attitude important in this process of overcoming fear?

Answer: Matthew 7:7, Jesus-Iu'sus said "...Seek and You Shall Find; Knock and it will be opened to you." What should we be seeking? According to what Jesus said in Matthew 6:33, first we should be striving for the kingdom of God and His righteousness. To overcome fear we must pray, have faith, live in righteousness, have good moral character, and our positive attitude of mind towards life will determine the road we are to travel; it is fear that cuts us off from our successes in life. If we expect nothing we shall have nothing; if we demand much we shall receive the greater portion. The world is harsh only because we fail to assert ourselves. The criticism of the world is bitter only to those who cannot compel room for their ideas. It is fear of this criticism that causes many ideas to fail to see the light of day.

Question: what about the people who don't know anything about the solar plexus, what will they do?

Answer: you have to go out and teach them about the great solar center within. **John 1: 9 9- The true light that gives light to everyone that comes into the world.**

For the man who knows that he has a Solar Plexus will not fear criticism or anything else; he will be too busy radiating courage, confidence, and power; he will anticipate success by his mental attitude; he will pound barriers to pieces and leap over the wall of doubt and hesitation which fear places in his path.

If we were to have knowledge of our ability to consciously radiate health, strength and harmony it would bring us into a realization that there is nothing to fear because we are in touch with **Infinite Strength of the Almighty Creator.**

This knowledge can be gained only by making a practical application of this information. We learn through action, by doing; it is through practice that the weight lifter becomes powerful.

As the following statement is of considerable importance, I will put it in several ways, so that you cannot fail to get the full significance of it. If you are religiously inclined, I would say, you can **let your true light shine.** If your mind has a bias

towards physical science, I would say **you can wake the Solar Plexus;** or, if you prefer the strictly scientific interpretation, I will say that you can impress your subconscious mind. If you are living a Kemetic Sacred life I would simply show you this symbol:

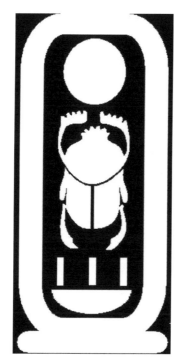

I AM BECOMING

HETEP

UNIVERSAL MIND OR DIVINE MIND

The subconscious mind is a part of the Universal mind or Divine Mind. The Universal- RA is the creative principle of the Universe, a part must be the same in kind and quality as the whole. (Neb-Er-Tcher – Neteru)

This means that this creative power is absolutely unlimited; it is not bound by precedent of any kind, and consequently has no prior existing pattern by which to apply its constructive principle.

We have found that the subconscious mind is responsive to our conscious will, which means that the unlimited creative power of the Universal Mind is within the control of the conscious mind of the individual.

When making a practical application of this principle, in accordance with the exercises given in Parts, it is important to remember that it is not necessary to outline the method by which the subconscious will produce the results you desire. The **finite** cannot inform the **Infinite**. You are simply to say what you desire, not how you are to obtain it.

You are the channel by which the undifferentiated is being differentiated, and this differentiation is being accomplished by appropriation. It only requires recognition to set causes in motion which will bring about results in accordance with your desire, and this is accomplished because the Universal can act only through the individual, and the individual can act only through the Universal; they are one.

Exercise One

Exercise one: I want you to not only be perfectly still, and inhibit all thought as far as possible, but relax, let go, let the muscles take their normal condition; this will remove all pressure from the nerves and eliminate tension which so frequently produces physical exhaustion.

Physical relaxation is a voluntary exercise of the will and the exercise will be found to be of great value, as it enables the blood to circulate freely to and from the brain and body.

Tension leads to mental unrest and abnormal mental activity of the mind; it produces worry, care, fear and anxiety. Relaxation is therefore an absolute necessity in order to allow the mental faculties to exercise the greatest freedom.

Make this exercise as thorough and complete as possible, mentally determine that you will relax every muscle and nerve, until you feel quiet and restful and at peace with yourself and the world.

The Solar Plexus will then be ready to function and you will be surprised at the result.

WHO ARE YOU?

What is it which controls that which you call yourself. "You" are not your body; the body is simply the physical instrument which the ego uses to carry out its purpose. "You" are not your mind; this is simply another instrument which the ego uses to think, reason and plan. When you say "'I' go" you tell the body where to go, when you say "'I' think" you tell the mind what to think. When you come into a realization of the true nature of the "I" you will enjoy a sense of power which nothing else can give, because you will come to know what you are, who you are, what you want, and how to get it.

THE KA OR PERSONALITY

What you think, or do, or feel, is an indication of what you are.

Thought is energy, and energy is power, and it is because all the religions, sciences and philosophies with which the world has heretofore been familiar have been based upon the manifestation of this energy instead of the energy itself, that the world has been limited to effects, while causes have been ignored or misunderstood.

DUALITY

For this reason we have **God** and the **Devil** in religion, **positive** and **negative** in science, and **good** and **bad** in philosophy.

The Kemetic Sacred Life reverses the process; it is interested only in **cause**, and **adepts** who are living the Kemetic Sacred Life are finding the cause and they are securing for themselves health, harmony, abundance, and whatever else may be necessary for their welfare and happiness.

Life is expressive and it is our business to express ourselves harmoniously and constructively. Sorrow, misery, unhappiness,

disease and poverty are not necessities and we need to constantly eliminate them.

But this process of eliminating consists of rising above and beyond limitation of any kind. He who has strengthened and purified his **thoughts** need not concern himself with material effects, because he who has come into an overstanding of the **law of abundance** will go at once to the Eternal Father, the source of **ALL** supply.

BE CARE OF THE "I", DEVELOP THE "I AM"

Question: what is the "I" in us all?

Answer: **the "I" in you is not the physical body;** that is simply an instrument which the "I" uses to carry out its purposes; **the "I" cannot be the Mind,** for the mind is simply another instrument which the "I" uses with which to think, reason, and plan.

The **"I"** controls and directs both the **body** and the **mind;** something which determines what they shall do and how they shall act. When you come into a realization of the true nature of the "I" you will enjoy a sense of **humble-power** which you have never before known.

The **KA** or personality is made up of countless individual characteristics, peculiarities, habits and traits of character; these are the result of your **former method of thinking,** but they have nothing to do with the real **"I."**

When you say "I think," the "I" tells the mind what it should think; when you say "I'm going," the "I" tells the physical body where to go; **the real nature of the "I" is spiritual,** and is the source of the real power which comes to us, when we come into the realization of our true nature which is spiritual.

The greatest and most marvelous power which the **"I"** has been given is the power to **think,** but few people know how to think constructively, or correctly, so most people achieve only indifferent results.

SELFISHNESS

Most people allow their thoughts to dwell on selfish purposes, but when a mind becomes mature, it overstands that the origin of defeat is in **every selfish thought.**

THE TRAINED MIND

The **trained mind** knows that every transaction must benefit every person who is in any way connected with the transaction, and any attempt to profit by the weakness, ignorance or necessity of another will inevitably operate to his disadvantage.

Question: why is that so?

Answer: because the **individual** is a part of the **Universal**, all things are universally connected. A part cannot work against another part and expect positive results; it has to work with other parts for the welfare and interests of the whole.

OVERSTANDING – STAND OVER KNOWLEDGE

Those who overstand and recognize this principle have a great advantage in the affairs of life. They do not wear themselves out with feetless thoughts. They have the ability to focus and concentrate on the highest possible degree on any subject. They do not waste time or money upon ideas and objects which can be of no possible benefit to them.

If you cannot do this it is because you do not overstand this principle, or have not made the necessary effort to learn it. Now is the time to make the effort. The result will be exactly in proportion to the effort expended.

Question: what is it that we need to learn, and how do we learn it or make the effort?

Answer: you need to learn how to strengthen the "WILL". Man's "will" has to be in accord with divine will, or the outer

self (mind) has to be in accord with the spiritual "inner self" or the "I AM". One of the strongest affirmations which you can use for the purpose of **"strengthening the inner self"**, or the "will" and realizing your latent power within is, **"through "I AM" I can be what I will to be."**

Question: what is the "I AM"?

Answer: the **"I AM" (Yah/Jah/Hu)** is God's name in man; it is **Yahuwa**, the indwelling **Karast-Christ, the true spiritual being** whom God made in His image and likeness. The outer, manifest man is the offspring of the I AM, or inner spiritual self. By use of I AM we make conscious union with the Source, the Father, with Spirit, with abiding life, wisdom, love, peace, substance, strength, power, Truth, and with the kingdom of the heavens within us.

Every time you repeat it realize who and what the true "I" is; try to come into a thorough overstanding of the true nature of the "I"; if you do you will become invincible; that is, provided that your objects and purposes are constructive and are therefore in harmony with the creative principle of the Universe. The "I" must connect with the "AM", the true self, and in turn the "I AM" with connect with the "I AM that I AM which is the Father, the source of "I AM". (YHWH)

YOU MUST FINISH WHAT YOU START

If you make use of this affirmation, use it continuously, night and morning, and as often during the day as you think of it, and continue to do so until it becomes a part of you; you will form a habit in mind.

If you start this affirmation process you must not stop it, because when we start something and do not complete it, or make a resolution and do not keep it, we are forming the habit of failure in our hearts and minds. If you do not intend to do a thing, do not start; if you do start, see it through even if the heavens fall; if you make up your mind to do something, do it; let nothing, or no one interfere with it; the "I" in you has determined, the thing is settled; the die is cast, there is no longer any argument, just do it!!

Question: Is the "I" the ego?

Answer: yes, the "I" is the ego which is necessary to act, and driver toward in life, but the "I" must be controlled by the "I AM", the spiritual "I".

Question: how do we start to control it?

Answer: If you carry out this idea, beginning with small things which you know you can control and gradually increase the effort, but never under any circumstances allow your "I AM" to be overruled, you will find that you can eventually control yourself, and many people have found to their sorrow that it is easier to control a kingdom than to control themselves. (See Lord of the rings)

SELF CONTROL

When you have learned to control yourself you will have found the **"World Within"** which controls the **world without**. This is the power that Iu'sus – Jesus showed the world, he controlled the **"inner and the outer worlds"**. (**Lord of the worlds**)

This is not so strange or impossible as it may appear when you remember that in man, the "World Within" is controlled by the "I AM" and that this "I AM" is a part or one with the Infinite "I Am that I AM" which is the Universal Energy or Spirit, usually called God. (YHWH) This was established in the mysteries, in the greatest religious thought, as well by the greatest scientific thought. This I Am that I Am is spiritual and scientific, it is called the strong and weak nuclear forces, the underlying power in all things.

Herbert Spencer said: "Amid all the mysteries by which we are surrounded, nothing is more certain than that we are ever in the

presence of an Infinite and Eternal Energy from which all things proceed." **Herbert Spencer was an English philosopher, biologist, anthropologist, sociologist, and prominent classical liberal political theorist of the Victorian era.**

Science goes a little way in its search and stops. Science finds the ever-present Eternal Energy, but Religion finds the Power behind this energy and locates it within man. But this is by no means a new discovery; the Bible says exactly the same thing:

Corinthians 3:16

Don't you know that you are God's temple and that God's Spirit lives in you?

Romans 8:9 you, however, are not in the realm of the flesh but are in the realm of the Spirit, if indeed the Spirit of God lives in you. And if anyone does not have the Spirit of Christ, they do not belong to Christ.

Corinthians 3:17 if anyone destroys God's temple, God will destroy that person; for God's temple is sacred, and you together are that temple.

1 Corinthians 6:19 Do you not know that your bodies are temples of the Holy Spirit, who is in you, whom you have received from God? You are not your own;

Hebrews 3:6 But Christ is faithful as the Son over God's house. And we are his house, if indeed we hold firmly to our confidence and the hope in which we glory.

POWER OF THE WORLD WITHIN

There is a great, powerful, sacred creative power of the "World Within."

Here is the hidden of power of mastery.

Question: should we go without things?

Answer: To overcome does not mean to go without things. Self-denial is not success. We cannot give unless we get; we cannot be helpful unless we are strong. The Infinite is not a bankrupt and we who are the representatives of Infinite power and we should not be bankrupts either, and if we wish to be of service to others we must have power, but to receive it we must give it; we must be of service.

The more we give the more we shall receive; we must become a channel whereby the Universal can express activity. The Universal is constantly seeking to express itself, to be of service, and it seeks the channel whereby it can find the greatest activity, where it can do the most good, where it can be of greatest service to humanity.

BE READY TO SERVE

The Universal (God) cannot express through you as long as you are busy with your plans, your own purposes; quiet the senses, seek inspiration, focus the mental activity within, dwell in the consciousness of your unity with Omnipotence. **"Still water runs deep";** contemplate the infinite opportunities to which you have spiritual access by the Omnipresence power of ALL.

VISUALIZE

Visualize the events, circumstances and conditions which these spiritual connections may assist in manifesting. Realize the fact that the essence and soul of all things is spiritual and that the spiritual is the real, because it is the life of all there is; when the spirit is gone, the life is gone; it is dead; it has ceased to exist.

MENTAL

These mental activities pertain to the world within, to the world of **cause;** and **conditions** and **circumstances** which result is the effect. So have to become a creator every day. This is important work, and the higher, loftier, grander and nobler the ideals which you can conceive, the more important the work will become.

SET LIMITS

Over-work or over-play or over-bodily activity of any kind produces conditions of **mental apathy and stagnation** which makes it impossible to do the more important work which results in a realization of conscious power. We should, therefore, seek Silence and **"TO BE STILL"** frequently.

Power comes through repose; it is in the Silence that we can be still, and when we are still we can think, and thought is the secret of all attainment.

TEHUTI – THOTH – THOUGHT - ACTION

Thought is a mode of motion and is carried by the law of vibration the same as light or electricity. It is given vitality by the emotions through the law of love; it takes form and expression by the law of growth; it is a product of the spiritual "I AM," which is **its Divine, spiritual, and creative nature**.

From this it is evident that in order to **express power,** abundance or any other constructive purpose, the emotions must be called upon to give feeling to the **thought** so that it will take form. How may this purpose be accomplished? This is the vital point; **how may we develop the faith, the courage, the feeling, which will result in accomplishment?**

EXERCISE AND MENTAL STRENGTH

By exercise, and mental strength is secured in exactly the same way that physical strength is secured, by mental exercise. We think something, perhaps with difficulty the first time; we think the same thing again, and it becomes easier the next time; we think it again and again; it then becomes a mental habit. We continue to think the same thing; finally it becomes automatic; we can no longer help thinking this thing; we are now positive of what we think; there is no longer any doubt about it. We are sure now, we don't think or believe, we know.

RELAX AND LET GO

I want you to practice this exercise every day. Now, I want you to relax, to let go physically. Now I am going to ask you to let go mentally. If you practice this exercise fifteen or twenty minutes a day, clearing your mind, you should be able to relax physically; **and anyone who cannot consciously do this quickly and completely is not a master of himself.** He has not obtained freedom; he is still a slave to conditions. But if you have mastered the exercise you are ready to take the next step, which is mental freedom.

Now after taking your usual position, remove all tension by completely relaxing, then mentally let go of all adverse conditions, such as hatred, anger, worry, jealousy, envy, sorrow, trouble or disappointment of any kind.

If you say you cannot "let go" of these things, you need a lot of work, but you can; you just have to make up your mind to do so, by voluntary intention and persistence.

The reason that some cannot do this is because they allow themselves to be controlled by their emotions instead of by their intellect. But the **will** guided by the **intellect** will gain the victory. The first time you try it may seem difficult, but keep practicing it until you master it. You must succeed in **dismissing, eliminating,** and **completely destroying** these negative and destructive thoughts; because they are the **seed** which is constantly germinating into discordant conditions of every conceivable kind and description.

Beginning

GENERAL QUESTIONS

1. Q: What is the world without in its relation to the world within? (Subjective to objective worlds)

A: The world without is a reflection of the world within.

2. Q; Upon what does all possession depend?

A: All possession is based on consciousness.

3. Q: How is the individual related to the objective world?

A: The individual is related to the objective world by the objective mind; the brain is the organ of this mind.

4. Q: How is the individual related to the Universal Mind?

A: The individual is related to the Universal Mind by the subconscious mind; the Solar Plexus is the organ of this mind.

5. Q: What is the Universal Mind or Divine Mind?

A: The Universal Mind or Divine Mind is the life principle of every atom which is in existence.

6. Q: How can the Individual act on the Universal?

A: The ability of the individual to think is his ability to act upon the Universal and bring it into manifestation.

7. Q: What is the result of this action and interaction?

A: The result of this action and inter-action is cause and effect; every thought is a cause, and every condition an effect.

Tehuti knotted with Heru symbolic of cause and effect

8. Q: How are harmonious and desirable conditions secured?

A: Harmonious and desirable conditions are obtained by right thinking.

9. Q: What is the cause of all discord, chaos, lack and limitation?

A: Discord, chaos, lack and limitation are the result of wrong thinking.

10. Q: What is the source of all power?

A: The source of all power is the world within, the Universal Fountain of Supply, the Infinite Energy of which each individual is an outlet.

11. Q: What are the two modes of mental activity?

A: Conscious and subconscious.

12. Q: Upon what do ease and perfection depend?

A: Ease and perfection depend entirely upon the degree in which we cease to depend upon the conscious mind.

13. Q: What is the value of the subconscious?

A: It is enormous; it guides us, warns us, it controls the vital processes and is the seat of memory.

14. Q: What are some of the functions of the conscious mind?

A: It has the faculty of discrimination; it has the power of reasoning; it is the seat of the will and may impress the subconscious.

15. Q: How has the distinction between the conscious and subconscious been expressed?

A:"Conscious mind is reasoning will. Subconscious mind is instinctive desire, which is the result of past reasoning will."

16. Q: What method is necessary in order to impress the subconscious?

A: Mentally state what is desired.

17. Q: What will be the result?

A: If the desire is in harmony with the forward movement of the great Whole, forces will be set in motion which will bring about the result.

18. Q: What is the result of the operation of this law?

A: Our environment reflects conditions corresponding to the predominant mental attitude which we entertain.

19. Q: What name has been given to this law?

A: The Law of Attraction.

20. Q How is the law stated?

A: Thought is a creative energy, and will automatically correlate with its object and bring it into manifestation.

In the Kemetic Mysteries Heru symbolizes cause, the "Will", the heart, and it is Tehuti who symbolizes effect, the "tongue", action. The thoughts of Heru are positive, divine thoughts of great character, but the thoughts of man may be positive or negative, never the less, the cause is as absolute and unchanging in the subjective realm as the effect of Tehuti is in the objective physical realm. Divine Mind is the master tailor, stitching together the interior lining of character and the outer fabric of manifest circumstance — **Tjeti Faheem Judah-EL.**

CAUSE & EFFECT

21. Q: What system of nerves is the organ of the Conscious Mind?

A: The Cerebro-spinal.

22. Q: What system of nerves is the organ of the subconscious mind?

A: The sympathetic.

23. Q; what is the central point of distribution for the energy which the body is constantly generating?

A: The solar plexus.

24. Q: How may this distribution be interrupted?

A: By resistant, critical, discordant thoughts, but especially by fear.

25. Q: What is the result of such interruption?

A: Every ill with which the human race is afflicted.

26. Q: How may this energy be controlled and directed?

A: By conscious thought.

27. Q: How may fear be completely eliminated?

A: By an overstanding and recognition of the true source of all power.

Q: 28. What determines the experiences with which we meet in life?

A: Our predominant mental attitude.

29. Q: How may we awake the solar plexus?

A: Mentally concentrate upon the condition which we desire to see manifested in our lives.

30. Q: What is the creative principle of the Universe?

A: The Universal Mind.

HOSEA 13:4

"Yet I am the LORD thy God from the land of Egypt, and thou shalt know no god but me: for there is no savior beside me."

TERMS

WORD - The only expression of Divine Mind is the Logos, or Word, the one universal Man–God. This is the Karast-Christ or anointed one. It is Mind manifest, and he who lets the "mind . . . which was also in "Christ Jesus- Karast Iu'su" be in him becomes the Son of God. As thought is the only mode of manifestation of Mind, it follows that the only way to accomplish such manifestation is to think the thoughts that we know correspond in purity and truth to the thought of God. Thoughts are things, which can be controlled and regulated. The thoughts of men ultimate in their bodies and environments. When men know this they will proceed to cultivate their

thoughts more carefully than they do their fields. By casting out by denial all undesirable thoughts and planting by affirmation all good thoughts, man will soon find himself surrounded by a universe of beauty and harmony only. All sin, sickness, poverty, and death will disappear. He will have a new body as light as air and as indestructible as electricity. This training of the mind results in habitual thinking of pure thoughts until finally the thinker slips like a crystal dewdrop into the flowing sea of pure thinking, the Logos or Word of Yahuwa-God. HUHI

WATER (TEFNUT) - Water in its different aspects represents weakness and negativity, cleansing, mental potentiality-Nun, and in some cases life, or vital energy. (Yin)

NUN - The waters of Genesis 1:6, 7 represent unexpressed possibilities in mind. There must be a firm starting point established. This point or **"firmament" is faith** moving on the unformed capacities of Spirit consciousness. (Infinite potential)

In every mental proposition we have an above and a below. Above the firmament are the unexpressed capacities (waters) of the conscious mind resting in faith in Divine Mind. Below the firmament are the unexpressed capacities (waters of the Nun) of the subconscious mind.

The "Seas" of Genesis 1:10 represent the unformed state of mind. We say that a man is "at sea" when he is in doubt about a

mental process; in other words he has not established his thoughts in line with the principle involved, he is unstable. The sea is capable of production, but must come under the dominion of the formative power of mind, the imagination.

Water ("the sea"), in Mark 6:47-51, represents mental potentiality; it can also be understood as negation. The race thoughts have formed a sea of thought, and to walk over it safely requires that one have faith in oneself. Faith necessary to accomplish so great a work comes from understanding-- of Yahu-God and man and the law of mastery given to man.

Yahuwa-God is substance: sub, under; stare, to stand. He is the underlying principle of the universe, upholding all things by His word of power, by the omnipresent energy that permeates all creation. An understanding of God in His true character establishes the mind firmly in faith and causes the feet to walk safely over the sea of the mixed, negative thoughts of the race.

It is not necessary to walk on material water to follow Jesus-Iu'su. His walking on the water is a lesson in spiritual overcoming. When we have found the spirit of the law the material expression adjusts itself. We live constantly in a sea of thought that is moved on by every impulse of the mind. There are greater storms on land than on sea, and they are far more destructive because of the many minds reached by the psychic

waves. Men need every day the saving call, "Be of good cheer: it is I; be not afraid."

The majority of men try to sail the ocean of life without the sustaining power of Spirit, but eventually they always go down in a troubled sea. Even those who have been taught of the Master are still filled with doubts and fears when storms arise, and instead of a reality they see an apparition. But the Karast-Christ mind is not an apparition; it is a mighty power, and when we have faith in it all the discordant elements of our life are quieted and we reduce to harmony and wholeness everything that our peace-giving thoughts touch.

Water, in one of its phases, represents negativity. The individual who allows himself to become negative to the good finds himself uncertain and unstable in his mind, and often his body becomes so submerged in the waters of negation that his physical condition is low. Weak sympathy with error and the results of error helps to produce this condition. To be positive in the good it is very necessary that one have right ideas of Yahuwa-God, that one knows Him as good. The mind and the body are often toned up by one's thinking of Yahuwa-God as divine law (Maat). One's understanding Him to be divine law frees the mind from sentimental ideas of Yahuwa-God solely as

love. It is these sentimental ideas that make weak human sympathy.

Yahuwa-God is our Father, and it is His place to instruct and discipline us in righteousness. Those who will not learn their lessons in easy ways will have to learn them in hard ways, and we should not be sentimentally sympathetic with those who make severe corrections necessary. Weak, teary sympathy is just one of the ways in which we bring floods upon ourselves. Water often breaks up and dissolves old error states of consciousness in the individual, just as the Flood dissolved and washed away from the race the old conditions that the combined error force of individuals had formed.

Water is symbolical of weakness, lack of stability: "Unstable as water, thou shalt not excel" (Gen. 49:4, A. V.). In Mark 14:13 it is stated that the disciples were to recognize the man in whose home they were to eat the Passover by his carrying a pitcher of water. The meaning is that we should meet the error thought at the weakest point in consciousness. The error thought to be met in this case was designated as Judas, one of the disciples, who was possessed of a devil. This means that Jesus had discovered that He had one point in His character that was not yet cleansed and spiritualized by the power of the word, or the regenerating thought given by the Father. He said on a former occasion that

His disciples (faculties) were all clean through the power of the word, save this one. So Jesus had to meet in the Judas faculty the reaction of an error thought that was working there from the personal or adverse side of existence.

Water also represents material cleansing, and fire represents spiritual cleansing. When John the Baptist baptized with water, he washed away the sins of an external character. He did not enter into the sub-consciousness. It takes something more powerful than water to purify the error conditions accumulated by the soul in its many incarnations. The presence of God through Christ is necessary to purify this part of man. (See BAPTISM.)

Water (TEFNUT) also represents the great mass of thoughts that conform to environment. Every thought leaves its form in the consciousness, and all the weak, characterless words and expressions gather in the subconscious mind as water gathers in holes. When we get discouraged or disappointed and "give up," the undertow of life sweeps this flood of negative thought over us, and we are conscious of bodily weakness of some sort. Then, if we get scared, there is trouble ahead. When we know the Truth, and "brace up," however, the waters are confined to their natural channels again and our strength is restored.

EARTH (GEB)- the earth represents the consciousness of the physical body.

FIRE – (SET) - fire--Symbolizes cleansing and purification, but it is more than a symbol. Material fire is the symbol, and the fire of Spirit is the reality. The whole universe is alive with a divine, living, spiritual energy that consumes all the dross of sense and materiality. It is a fire that burns eternally. Because this is true, some have assumed that disobedient, sinful persons are to live forever in everlasting torment, but if the fire is eternal, the dross is not, and when the error is consumed the burning stops. The fire consumes only when it meets anything unlike itself. In purified man it is manifested as his eternal life.

Fire of God--The Word of God in action. It burns out the dross of negative consciousness and reveals the Christ.

Fire (SET), tongues of--Illumination of thought, in demonstration of Spirit's presence and power.

Air—(SHU) The deific breath of God. It symbolizes a purifying, vitalizing power that revives and makes alive.

Ground, holy--Substance in its spiritual wholeness, or the idea of substance in Divine Mind. When we realize this idea we let go of all limitation and are conscious only of the Absolute.

Elohim God--The original Mind in creative action. El means "the strong and ever-sustaining one," and Allah, "to swear or formulate by the power of the Word." Elohim thus represents the universal Principle of Being that designed all creation.

Yahweh--The original Hebrew form of Jehovah. It means "the self-existent one" who reveals Himself to His creation and through His creation.

Yahweh, Yahuwa, HuHi revealed Himself to Jesus-Iu'su as the Father within; Yahweh revealed himself to Moses as "I AM THAT I AM" (Exod. 3:14).

Tabernacle – tabernacle represents the temporal body of man, as the Temple built by Solomon in Jerusalem represents the permanent body. In the wilderness of sense, man worships Yahuwa-God in a tent, or a temporary, transitory state of mind, which makes a perishable body. Yet in this flimsy structure are all the furnishings of the great temple that is to be built. So the body of every man is the promise of an imperishable one.

THE SON OF YAHUWA-GOD - Son of God--The fullness of the perfect-man idea in Divine Mind, the Karast-Christ. The true spiritual self of every individual. The living Word; the Karast-Christ idea in the Mind of Yahuwa-God.

The Son ever exists in Infinite-God. Father and Son are one and are omnipresent in man and the universe. Jesus (Iu'sus) represents God's idea of man in expression (Son of man); Christ is that idea in the Absolute (Son of God). The Christ is the man that God created in His image and likeness, the perfect-idea man. He is the real self of all men.

Blessed are they which do hunger and thirst after righteousness

Tjeti Faheem Judah-EL

Faheem Judah-EL is an innovative thinker and teacher; he is a world traveler, spiritual teacher, metaphysician, writer, publisher, researcher, and meditation guide. Faheem has studied many spiritual disciplines such as The Egiptian Mysteries, The Greater Mysteries, Christianity, The Lesser Mysteries, The Ethiopian Mysteries, Metaphysics, Arabic, Hebrew, Sumerian Theology, Natural Health, The Dogon Mystery Tradition, Sufi Traditions, The Medu Neter, Kundilini Chakra System, Life of Christ-Heru. He has written and published many books on

spiritual concepts. Mr. Judah-EL has traveled to many parts of the world such as: Ethiopia, Egipt, Mecca, Mexico, Kenya, South Africa, Uganda and many Native American Mound Centers of North America. As a meditation Guide he has helped many people learn how to reduce stress and develop the spiritual self within.

NOTES

KEMETIC HOLISTIC LIFE COACHING 101

KEMETIC HOLISTIC LIFE COACHING 101

ISBN

978-1-304-15887-1

Axum Publication

Decatur Illinois 62521

www.lulu.com/egipt

Made in the USA
Middletown, DE
19 September 2018